Established In The Gospel

A Study Designed to Help Christians Be Solid in the Faith

By
Tom Elliott

Fort Collins, Colorado

Romans 16:25-27 "Now to him who is able to establish you by my gospel and the proclamation of Jesus Christ, according to the revelation of the mystery hidden for long ages past, but now revealed and made known through the prophetic writings by the command of the eternal God, so that all nations might believe and obey him - to the only wise God be glory forever through Jesus Christ! Amen. [NIV]

Established in the Gospel

Published by: Walk With God Publishing
WalkWithGod.org

ISBN Printed Book: 978-1507640241

Visit: JesusFocused.com to find more books and study materials by Tom Elliott

TABLE OF CONTENTS

REGISTER THIS BOOK

Get access to more study materials by visiting:
http://bit.ly/establishedinthegospel

INTRODUCTION

Welcome to the greatest adventure… Walking with God. That's right, it is an adventure. What could be more exciting than getting to know God? The Creator of the universe has summoned you into His Kingdom and you will find His Kingdom to be much different than the current world system. Therefore it is important for you to be established in some of the foundational truths of God's Kingdom. You may be brand new to the ways of God, returning to your first love or just getting reacquainted with God. Nevertheless, it's critical for you to have a strong foundation, which nothing can move.

That is the purpose for this study. God has designed the Christian life to be one of victory. Unfortunately, many Christians never discover the victorious life. This is due to many factors such as not understanding grace, lack of spiritual discipline, legalism, and even false teaching. Whatever the case, it is a tragedy, especially in light of what Jesus said life was meant to be in John 10:10: *The thief comes only to steal and kill and destroy; I have come that they may have life, and have it to the full.*

By no means would I want to mislead any of you into thinking that this means your life will be void of suffering. Not at all, Jesus also said in John 16:33: *I have told you these things, so that in me you may have peace. In this world you will have trouble. But take heart! I have overcome the world.* This is the difference, Jesus has overcome the world and with Him, we overcome as well. This is what He wants for you, to overcome. Jesus did not die on a Cross and rise from the dead to help you just "get by." He destined you for a life of overcoming sin, influencing others, and knowing Him as a Friend. I pray you will be diligent in these studies, so that you may be *Established in the Gospel.*

CHAPTER 1
WHAT HAS HAPPENED TO ME?

You have made the most important decision in your life, the decision to walk with God. I am sure your decision to become a follower of Jesus was made with seriousness; after all this is not like deciding what kind of car to drive... this is your life both now and forever. Jesus calls us and asks us to give up all to follow Him. In return He gives back far more than we could ever imagine. You have begun a journey of marvelous discoveries and with each new discovery you will find it to be a treasure of immeasurable depth. Each truth of the Christian faith can be understood to some degree at first, but new meaning of that truth will unfold for the rest of your life. Every serious Christian who has walked with God even for decades will tell you that they are constantly discovering beautiful nuances of even the most basic truths.

Since you have given your life to Christ you may be wondering, "Just how am I different than before?" Good question. I believe you will be amazed at what the Bible says about this.

Read John 3:3

1. What is required to be in the Kingdom of Heaven?

Read Ephesians 2:8-9 and Titus 3:4-5

2. According to these verses what are we saved by?

3. What cannot save us?

4. Is salvation a gift or is it earned?

Read Romans 3:10-12 and 21-24

5. Why can we not earn our salvation?

6. Does it appear that man is good or evil?

7. Do you agree with vs. 23, which says, "All have sinned?"

Read Romans 6:23

8. What are the wages of sin?

9. What is the gift of God?

Let's take a test to see just how sinful we are. The subject matter is the 10 commandments. These are the primary laws that governed the Hebrew people of the Old Testament. The test is this: how many of them have you kept? Now remember, to keep one means you have gone your entire life without even the smallest violation.

- You shall have no other gods but the one true God.

- You shall not worship any idol (person, thing, job, self, etc.)

- You shall not take the Lord's name in vain (this not only means cursing, but making His name common).

- You shall honor the Sabbath day and keep it holy.

- You shall honor your Father and Mother (every day)?

- You shall not murder (before you think you finally got one please read Matthew 5:21-22)

- You shall not commit adultery (again before you chalk one up read Matthew 5:27-28)

- You shall not steal.

- You shall not lie.

- You shall not covet something that belongs to another (this can include jealousy).

Well, how did you do? Please don't be discouraged with your results, you will find most of us don't even come close. The point being made is this: we are far from the standard God established for His people to follow. So when the Bible says all have sinned, it means what it says. This is why we cannot save ourselves. This is why we need to be born again.

Let's now look at some of the changes that have occurred in your life since you gave your life to Jesus.

Read Colossians 1:13-14

10. What Kingdom did you previously belong to?

11. What Kingdom do you belong to now and what are some of the benefits?

Read II Corinthians 5:17-21

12. According to vs. 17, what has happened to you?

13. In your own words, explain vs. 21.

Spend time thanking the Lord for this wonderful gift of New Life. It may seem too good to be true that you are now the "righteousness of God," but those are God's Words. You may not feel like it all the time, as a matter of fact if left to your feelings you will never believe it. But, the fact of the matter is that when Jesus does a job, it is done well.

CHAPTER 2
GRACE - SAVES AND TRANSFORMS

In 1987 I heard a message by a great preacher, EV Hill. He explained 2 Corinthians 5:21 in a way that changed my life. He explained that our "position" before God is that we are totally righteous because of Christ. Let's look at this verse again; "God made him who had no sin to be sin for us, so that in him we might become the righteousness of God." NIV – The truth of this verse is amazing. Lets break it down:

"God made him who had no sin" – This is Jesus.

"To be sin for us" – Jesus became sin on the Cross and paid the penalty of sin; death. He paid our penalty.

"So that in him we might become the righteousness of God" – Our sinfulness is exchanged for His righteousness.

On that day in 1987 I realized like never before that I was as righteous as Jesus was righteous. This almost sounds blasphemous, but to deny this truth is to deny scripture and to deny what Christ did on the Cross, which is blasphemous.

Pastor Hill went on to talk about our "condition." While our "position" is righteous because of Christ, our condition is a different story. None of us become like Jesus (in our daily conduct) the moment we are saved, we begin a lifelong process called sanctification. Sanctification is the process of our "condition" becoming like our "position." Pastor Hill then explained that if we trust God and believe that our "position" is completely righteous, then we will find it much easier to see our "condition" change into one of Christ like behavior. Friend, please get this… it will change your life, it is a universal truth that we live up too what we believe.

What many Christians fail to comprehend is that grace not only saves us, grace also transforms us. In other words, we are saved by grace and sanctified (transformed) by grace.

Saving Grace

1. Review 2 Corinthians 5:21, Ephesians 2:8-9 and Titus 3:4-5.

Read Romans 5:6-11

1. In what condition were we when Christ died for us? See vs. 6,8,10

2. What have we received according to vs. 11?

3. Spend time thanking God for saving you through Jesus.

4. Remember this acronym – GRACE; God's Riches At Christ's Expense.

Transforming Grace

Read Titus 2:11-14 and John 1:14

1. What does it mean that the "Grace of God has appeared?" (Do you think this is connected to Jesus being full of Grace and Truth?)

2. What does Grace "train" us to do?

3. According to vs. 14, what is Jesus working in us?

Most Christians know that they are saved by grace, but they may not realize that it is also grace which transforms us. Perhaps they believe that once God saves them then they are on their own.

This is a tragedy. We are just as helpless to be changed as we are to be saved. There is only one Person who ever walked this Earth and perfectly obeyed God, and that was Jesus. Jesus is the only one who can live the Christian life, and Jesus will live His life through you!

Read Colossians 1:27-29

1. What is the "hope of Glory?" (Glory in this case refers to Christians becoming more and more like God).

2. According to vs. 28, what was the main message of the Author of Colossians (Paul)?

Read 2 Peter 1:3-11

1. According to vs. 3, how many things have we been given for our life and to be godly? Is it some things, half of what we need or all things?

2. According to vs. 4, what do we get to participate in?

3. Look at vs. 5-7, what are the 7 characteristics we are told to pursue?

4. If we have already been given all things in vs. 3, how do we understand the command to pursue these characteristics?

5. According to vs. 9, what is the reason a Christian would lack these qualities?

The above passage captures this idea that Grace not only saves us, but also transforms us. In vs. 3 we have all things for life and godliness (this is by grace). When we believe this truth, we then see the qualities in vs. 5-7 not as things we need to receive but instead, characteristics we already have that get to be walked out. The only reason we would not grow in these characteristics is if we "forget that we have been cleansed of our sins." So it is not a matter of effort in which we grow in maturity, it an issue of faith… believing in what God has already given us.

I came up with this definition of grace some time ago; "Grace is power from God so that we can love God, obey God and serve

God." Dear friend... get this and you will walk in rest, peace, and victory.

Read 2 Peter 3:18

1. Did you notice that this is the last verse of the book? Do you think it is significant that the Apostle Peter closes out all of his writing with this truth?

Read Revelation 22:21

1. Why do you think that this is the last verse of the entire Bible?

CHAPTER 3
REPENTANCE

You mean when I become a Christian I have to change? You've got it! But a better way to put it is that you get to change. You get to change from anxiety to peace, selfishness to being generous, and from fear to security. Change is one of the constants of the Christian life and repentance is all about change. It means a change of mind, attitude, and behavior and it is something you will be doing the rest of your life. The reason for this is that as you fall more in love with God, you will in no way want to distance yourself from Him. You see, repentance means that you're not just sorry for your sin; rather you are sorry enough to quit. Repentance is a beautiful gift from God and as you will see, it's a doorway to many blessings in Christ. In this lesson we will look at the initial phases of repentance as well as some of the advanced parts.

Read Romans 8:29

1. Who are we destined to be like?

2. Will this require a great deal of change in your life?

Read Acts 2:36-38

3. Who did Peter say Jesus was in vs. 36?

4. What was the response of those who were listening?

5. What did Peter tell them to do?

6. What promises would they receive?

Read Luke 19:1-10

7. How did this man respond to Jesus?

8. Not only did this man change, but also made restitution for any money he had stolen. Why?

Read Ezekiel 33:15

9. What are some reasons God wants us to make restitution?

Read Luke 15:11-32

10. What condition was the young man in after being in the world for a time?

11. What did he decide to do?

12. How did his Father respond to him?

13. What blessing did he receive in response to his repentance?

Read II Corinthians 6:14-18

14. What do you think it means to not be yoked with unbelievers? *(Yoked means to participate in their way of living, just as an animal is yoked to another.)*

15. What does vs. 16 tell us we are?

16. In vs.18, what promise are you given if you obey vs.17?

Read I John 2:15-17

17. Why are we commanded not to love the world?

18. What is in the world?

19. What promise is given to those who do the will of God?

Read Acts 3:19

20. What promises do you receive when you "repent and turn to God?"

CHAPTER 4
BAPTISM

One of the most exciting steps of obedience in the Christian Life is baptism. In the case of baptism, or any aspect of God's Kingdom, it is vital to look to the Bible for guidance and not man's opinion. Some of you may have already said, "I don't need to study this, I have already been baptized." Well, in this study we will discover keys to how baptism can be a lifestyle as well as a one-time act. Also, it's important that you know how to teach others about baptism because Jesus told us to "Make disciples, baptizing them…"

Read Matthew 3:13-17

1. Why was Jesus baptized?

2. If Jesus needed to be baptized, then do you?

Read Mark 16:15-16

3. What must I do before I am baptized? *Hint: it's not preach, this would be after.*

Read Acts 2:38

4. Along with repentance, what were they commanded to do?

Read Acts 8:26-39

5. What did this man do when he believed the message of Christ?

6. What way or method was he baptized?

Read Acts 8:12

7. What did the people of Samaria do when they believed Philip's teaching?

Read Acts 16:29-34

8. What did the Philippian Jailer do when he believed Paul's message?

Spiritual Benefits of Baptism

Read Galatians 3:27

9. With who are we clothed when we are baptized?

10. What do you think this means?

Read I Peter 3:18-22

11. What Old Testament event is linked with baptism?

12. In vs. 21, what do we receive through obeying the command of baptism? *Notice it is faith in the resurrection of Jesus which is the source of our salvation.*

Read Genesis 17:10-11

13. What was circumcision a sign of in the Old Testament?

Read Philippians 3:3

14. Who did Paul say are the true circumcision?

Read Deuteronomy 30:6

15. How did Moses describe true circumcision?

Read Colossians 2:11-13

16. What act in these verses is compared to circumcision?

17. What do you think is meant by the removal of the flesh?

18. Who is the one who does this work?

Read I Corinthians 10:1-2

19. Why do you think the event of the Hebrew people passing through the Red Sea would be linked with baptism?

Read Exodus 14

20. From what kind of lifestyle were they being delivered?

21. How does this compare with our being baptized?

Read Romans 6:1-7

22. In your own words describe how the act of baptism is like the death and resurrection of Jesus.

23. What promises do we receive in these verses?

CHAPTER 5
THE AUTHORITY OF GOD'S WORD

There is no other book in the world like the Bible. It truly is a living document. It's more than good history, fascinating stories, or practical wisdom; it's an expression of the character of God. In this brief study we'll look at two primary aspects of God's Word. One is the place of God's Word in the life of a believer and the other is the many benefits of living according to the Word of God.

As you look up these scriptures you will find several different words used to describe the Bible: Law, Word, precepts, statutes, and scriptures are all used to indicate the Bible. Please don't get discouraged if you find things in the Bible you can't understand, this is common for all of us. After all, these Words have eternal meaning; they truly are the Words of an Infinite Being. (This chapter is a brief overview. In my book, *Grounded in the Word*, I help the reader understand how to properly use the Bible and how they can connect with God on a deeper level.) http://jesusfocused.com/shop/

Read II Timothy 3:16-17

1. What is the origin of Scripture?

2. What are the benefits of scripture to a Christian?

Read Matthew 4:4

3. What does man need to live on?

4. Was he speaking of physical or spiritual life?

Read Psalm 1

5. What is the outcome for one who meditates on God's Word day and night?

Read Proverbs 4:20-22

6. What approach are we to take with God's Word?

7. What are the blessings listed here?

Meditation is more than just casually reading, it is the diligent seeking of revelation and insight for daily living. We all meditate on something, but it's imperative that we allow the Lord to help us make His Word be that which feeds our souls continually. See Psalm 19:14.

Read Psalm 19

8. List the many ways God's Word blesses our lives. *Key in on vs. 7-11.*

Read Psalm 119:11

9. What word is used to describe this persons approach to the Word?

10. What will happen if we hide God's Word in our hearts?

Read Psalm 119:45

11. How will you walk about, if you obey the Word?

12. What do you believe this means?

Read Psalm 119:89

13. How is the Word described here?

Read Psalm 119:105

14. What do you think this verse means?

Read Psalm 119:136

15. How do lovers of God's Word feel when it is disobeyed?

16. Why?

Read Psalm 119:165

17. What are the two benefits of these verses?

Read Romans 12:2

18. How is our mind renewed?

Read Ephesians 5:26-27

19. What does the Word do for us according to this passage?

Read Ephesians 6:17

20. In terms of Spiritual armor, what is the Word called?

Read Matthew 4:4, 7, 10

21. How did Jesus respond when tempted by the devil?

Read Hebrews 4:12-13

22. Give a description of this sword.

Read Matthew 7:24-27

23. How would you describe the wise man and his house?

24. How would you describe the foolish man and his house?

Read Luke 8:21

25. Who did Jesus call his mother and brothers?

Read John 14:23

26. What is one way you can know if you really love Jesus?

Read Job 23:12

27. How important was the Word to this man?

CHAPTER 6
WHERE DOES CHRIST LIVE NOW?

I believe the following lesson to be one of the most glorious truths of the Christian Life. When believers in God come to understand that He is not just a deity who lives far away, but lives in their hearts, life is revolutionized. This is one of the most glorious truths and at the same time, mysterious. How can the God who created the stars, the human eye, and the human brain out of nothing, live inside of me? It may seem too good to be true, but it's true! Let's look at His Word to find out. (This chapter will help you better understand chapter 2, and how it is grace which transforms us).

Read II Chronicles 6:18-21

1. In this passage, where did God live?

2. What cannot contain God?

Read Jeremiah 31:33

3. Where will God write the Law?

Read Ezekiel 36:26, 27

4. Where will God put his Spirit?

Read Acts 17:24

5. Where does God no longer dwell?

Read I Corinthians 6:19

6. What is the new Temple of God?

Read Romans 8:9-11

7. How many times does the phrase "in you" occur in these verses?

8. What different terms are used to describe who is in you?

9. What blessings are found in this reality?

Read Galatians 2:20

10. Where does Christ live?

11. What are the results of this?

Read Colossians 1:24-29

12. Vs. 26 speaks of a mystery hidden for ages and generations; according to vs. 27 what is this mystery?

13. In light of all the other passages you have studied, why was this a mystery? *Look at this in light of the Old Testament passages you read earlier.*

Read II Corinthians 13:5

14. We are to examine ourselves to know if what is occurring in our lives.

15. How do we know if we are in the faith?

Read II Chronicles 7:1-3

16. What came down from heaven on the sacrifice?

17. In what building did this occur?

Read Acts 2:1-4

18. What was on the top of the heads of the 120 gathered in that room?

19. According to Acts 17:24 and I Corinthians 6:19 what "building" did this happen too?

In the Old Testament God dwelled in the Temple and when it was dedicated He came down with fire for the inauguration. In the New Testament God dwells in the hearts of men and women, and when it was dedicated He sent fire for the inauguration. This was and is the fulfillment of the passages you read in Ezekiel and Jeremiah. The wonderful news is this, you now live in an age when the "mystery has been revealed"—Christ lives in you and this is the hope of glory. Praise the Lord!

CHAPTER 7
FAITH IN GOD

Faith can be the most simple and at the same time the deepest of God's truths. Christianity is a venture of faith. While it's true that there is much historical, textual, and archaeological evidence for the Bible and the faith it promotes, no one has ever seen God in all His glory. First of all, no human can see God as He is and live. Secondly, faith is not faith if it is as clear as day. There would be no mystery or any reason to seek after God with all our hearts if there were no realm of faith. In this study we will look at some of the dimensions of faith, which will serve as just a small appetizer for a lifetime of seeking God with faith for even more faith.

Hebrews 11 is known as the faith chapter of the Bible. Most of this study will be based on this passage. Please read the entire chapter and then begin to answer the following questions. Before you read chapter 11, take a look at Hebrews 12:2. (In 2017, I will release *Walking by Faith*, in which I go into depth on this subject.) http://jesusfocused.com/shop/

Read Hebrews 12:2

1. Who is the Author of Faith? What does this mean?

2. Who is the Finisher of faith? What does this mean?

Before diving into this study, it is important to lay a foundation that faith is not of our making it is a gift from God. Jesus authors it, and finishes it. Knowing this will protect you from frustration and pride.

Read Hebrews 11

1. According to vs. 1, what is faith?

2. How did God create the Universe? Vs. 3

3. Can anyone please God apart from faith? Vs. 6

4. In your own words, describe how we must come to God, and what He does for those who earnestly seek Him?

5. How did Noah express his faith in God? Vs. *7 If you're not familiar with the story of Noah, see Genesis 6-10.*

6. How do you think Noah appeared to his contemporaries?

7. How did Abraham express his faith in God? Vs. 8-12

8. In vs. 16 why is God not ashamed to be called their God?

9. How did Moses express his faith in God? Vs. 23-29

10. What acts of power were performed by faith? Vs. 32-35

11. What acts of suffering did people of faith go through? Vs. 35-39

Read Ephesians 2:8

12. Through what are we saved?

Read Romans 10:8-10, 13, 14, 17

13. What actions do we perform to receive faith to be saved?

14. According to vs. 17, how does faith come into our lives?

Faith is more than head knowledge, it's a conviction of the heart. This is much deeper than just knowing the facts, it is a living demonstration of belief, just because God said it is true. We will now look at a few scriptures which show us this difference.

Read John 20:24-29

15. What kept Thomas from believing that Jesus was alive?

16. What made him believe?

17. What did Jesus say to him (and us) about belief? Vs. 29

Read Romans 4:17-22

18. Describe Abraham's faith from these verses.

19. According to vs. 17 what is God able to do? How does this relate to faith?

Read Matthew 6:33

20. How does this relate to faith?

21. What are the benefits of this kind of faith?

CHAPTER 8
THE CENTRALITY OF JESUS

This study could be as long as you want it to be. After all, Jesus is the main message of the Bible. For example, I hold in my hand a 528-page book devoted to prophecies concerning Jesus. The point is this; it will take all of this life just to scratch the surface of the greatness of Jesus, *"If all Jesus did were recorded in detail, there would not be enough books in the world."* (John 21:25)

Yes, He is *"beautiful beyond description and too marvelous for words."* Jesus must be the focus of your walk with God. You may have just read that and said, "That makes sense." However, you will find many Churches that emphasize a certain doctrine, practice, or belief system more than they emphasize the Lord Himself. Doctrine and these other things are vital but they can never replace Jesus. If they do in your life, you will have religion, but very little life. The first verse you will look at in this study is to me one of the most important in the Bible. It gives a summary of what the Christian life is all about.

Read Hebrews 12:1-3

1. How does sin hinder and entangle us?

2. Who are we to fix our eyes on?

3. What two names are given to Jesus in this passage? Vs. 2

4. What did this Author and Finisher of Faith do?

5. Where is He seated now?

6. Why are we to consider Him when we go through difficult times? Vs.3

Read Philippians 2:5-11

7. What should our attitude be like?

8. What nature does Jesus possess? Vs. 6

9. What nature did He take on? Vs. 7, 8

10. How much did He humble Himself? Vs. 8

11. What place is He now exalted to, since the Cross? Vs 9

12. Either voluntarily or involuntarily, what will every knee do, and what will every tongue confess someday?

Read Colossians 1:13-22

13. What are the promises in vs. 13-14?

14. Describe His characteristics in vs. 15-17.

15. Who is the Head of the Church? Vs. 18

16. How does He in all things have supremacy? Vs. 18

17. All of whose fullness dwells in Jesus? Vs. 19

18. List all the ways the Cross has reconciled all things and you as well. Vs. 20-22

Read Colossians 2:2-3

19. What treasures are found in Christ?

Read Colossians 3:1-4

20. Who have we been raised with?

21. Where are we to set our hearts and minds?

22. Who is our life hidden with?

23. Who is your life?

Read Colossians 3:17

24. In what name are we to do all things?

Read Isaiah 9:6, 7

25. List the attributes, accomplishments and names given for Jesus in this prophetic passage?

Read Isaiah 11:1-5

This is a Prophetic passage about Jesus. It lists many of characteristics and what the Spirit of God within Him would do.

26. List the Seven "spirits" of the Lord. *The first one is called "Spirit of the Lord, followed by the description "shall rest." This shows us that "rest" is a characteristic of Jesus as opposed to stress. List the other six characteristics.*

27. What will be the nature of His reign? Vs. 3-5

Read Revelation 1:8-18

28. List as many names, characteristics and attributes of Jesus you can.

CHAPTER 9
THE MINISTRY OF THE HOLY SPIRIT

You are not alone. God has provided you with the best help in the Universe; His very own Spirit. God the Father, God the Son, and God the Holy Spirit are one and yet three distinct Persons. You may remember from the earlier study on "Where does Christ live now," that He lives in you. In this study we will learn that the Holy Spirit lives in us as well. Since the Holy Spirit and Jesus walk in complete unity we can expect them to say the same things. In this study we will discover some of the benefits and blessings of the Holy Spirit living in your life. (This chapter is a brief overview, in my book *Guided by the Holy Spirit*, I go into many characteristics of the Holy Spirit and discuss how He can be your best friend.) http://jesusfocused.com/shop/

Read Acts 2:38

1. What two blessings do you receive after repentance and baptism?

Read Ephesians 1:13-14

2. What seal were you marked with?

3. What does this guarantee?

Read Romans 8:1-17

4. According to vs. 4, we no longer live according to what?

5. In vs. 5-6 what is the difference between those who have the Holy Spirit and those who do not?

6. In vs. 11, what promise do we have?

7. According to vs. 13, how can we "put to death" sinful behavior?

8. According to vs. 14, what is a characteristic of "Sons of God?"

9. In vs. 15 we find out we are no longer a slave to what?

10. What is our relationship to God now, what can we call Him? Vs. 15, 16

Read John 15:26

11. What does this say about the Holy Spirit as a Person?

Read John 16:13

12. What will He do for you?

Read Acts 13:2

13. In what way did the Holy Spirit operate in this situation?

Read I Thessalonians 5:19

14. What can happen to the Holy Spirit?

Read Acts 5:3, 4; I Corinthians 2:10; Hebrews 9:14

15. What attributes of Deity does He possess?

Read Matthew 3:16; John 3:8; John 7:37-38

16. What are some symbols attributed to Him?

Read John 14:16-31

17. As you read through this, write down the various ways the Holy Spirit will work in your life.

Read John 16:5-15

18. What are some other names for the Holy Spirit?

19. In what ways will He minister to you?

20. What will He do for Jesus? Vs. 14

Read Acts 1:8

21. What can you expect when the Holy Spirit comes upon you?

Read Acts 2:4

22. What happened to these early followers of Jesus?

Read Ephesians 5:18

23. What are we commanded to do in this passage?

Note: This command is written in its original language in such a way as to indicate that being filled with the Holy Spirit is a continual action. This should be understood to mean not more of the Holy Spirit, instead more of Him filling our lives. In other words, He does not come into our lives in segments, rather He waits for us to continue to surrender to His Lordship, and then more of his qualities become apparent in our lives. Please read 2 Peter 1:3 and you will see we have been given everything we need for life and godliness. This is another one of those paradoxes of the Christian life. We are filled with the Holy Spirit, yet we continually need to be filled with the Holy Spirit.

Read Romans 5:5

24. What quality does the Holy Spirit pour into our lives?

Read Galatians 5:16-26

25. What two powers are at war in your soul?

26. What are characteristics of the flesh?

27. What are the fruit of the Spirit?

28. Do you think it significant that they are called fruit and not fruits?

Note: This is significant, when we realize the truth of 2 Peter 1:3. These are given as a total package. This means within each one of us is love, joy, peace, etc. We may not see it now, but He will bring it forth in our lives.

CHAPTER 10
JESUS IS COMING AGAIN!

We live in a time of transition, a transition between the age of sin and the age of the glory of the Kingdom of God. This Earth began as a habitation for God and His people but it quickly became, through man's rebellion, a habitation of wickedness.

But it is God's full intention to see that everything He created is completely redeemed, and the price for this redemption has already been paid. When Jesus died on the Cross and rose from the grave He paid for both sin and death. These two enemies of God are the cause of all pain and grief.

So in the meantime, and it is often a "mean" time, man has the choice of following the ways of God or his own ways. The day is coming soon when Jesus will come again to rightfully take what already belongs to Him. When this day comes it will mean great despair for those who refuse Him, but joy of the greatest magnitude for His followers. Let's look at just a few of the scriptures, describing these days.

Read Acts 1:9-11

1. What did the angels promise these disciples of Jesus?

2. In what way will Jesus come back?

Read Matthew 24:29-31

3. Describe the nature of events just prior to His return.

4. How is His coming described in this passage?

Read I Thessalonians 4:13-18

Note: To understand this passage, know that "fallen asleep" is referring to death.

5. Who will come with Jesus when He returns?

6. Describe in your own words what the return of Jesus will be like.

7. In light of this, what are we to do for one another? Vs. 18

Read I Corinthians 15:51-58

8. What will happen to our bodies when Christ returns?

9. What enemy will be swallowed up in victory?

Read Revelation 1:7-8

10. What are the names of Jesus in these verses?

Read Revelation 19:11-16

11. How is Jesus described in this passage?

12. What are some of His names?

13. What will happen to those who did not follow him?

Read Revelation 21:1-8

14. What is God going to re-create?

15. How will God live with His people?

16. According to vs. 4, what things will be taken away forever?

17. What will happen to those who rebel against Jesus? Vs. 8

Read Revelation 22:7, 12, 13, 20

18. When is Jesus coming?

Read I Thessalonians 5:1-11

19. In light of His coming, how should we live?

Read Matthew 24:42-51

20. What is his return compared to? Vs. 43

21. How does the wise servant live in preparation for His master's return?

CHAPTER 11
THE MARK OF A CHRISTIAN

Of all the characteristics of God the most outstanding is His love. It will take all of eternity just to understand a fraction of this attribute.

Because the goal of the Holy Spirit is to make us like Christ, and since Jesus walked in perfect love, love is the main characteristic He will form in us. I believe every difficult situation is an opportunity to learn to love like God loves. Francis Schaeffer calls love the "mark of a Christian." Modern culture has done its best to cheapen love while God sees it as a priceless treasure. Let's take some time to study a few key passages about this boundless attribute. (This is a brief study; in late 2017 or early 2018 I will release *Living by Love*). http://jesusfocused.com/shop/

Read I Corinthians 13

1. How does this passage speak to you the first time you read it?

2. In vs.1-3, what gifts of the Holy Spirit is love greater than?

3. In verses 4-7 there are fifteen descriptions of love. Take time to list each one of these and write to the side what you think this means.

Read Psalm 103

4. In what ways does God show His people His love? List as many as you can.

5. Which three mean the most to you at this time in your life?

Read Galatians 5:6

6. How does faith properly express itself?

Read Philippians 1:9-10

7. What does he pray will abound more and more in knowledge and depth of insight?

8. What will result in our lives as this takes place?

Read Ephesians 3:14-21

9. In vs. 17, what does he pray we will be rooted and grounded in?

10. What does Christ's love surpass?

11. Why do you think knowing Christ's love surpasses just having a head knowledge of Him?

Read I John 3

12. Write down your observations about love from the following verses.

Vs. 1:

Vs. 10-12:

Vs. 14-18:

Vs. 23-24:

Read I John 4:7-21

13. Where does love come from?

14. How has God shown His love to us? Vs. 9

15. Who loved first, us or God?

16. Since God loves us, what should we do? Vs. 11

17. By what attribute can we see God in each other? Vs. 12

18. What do we come to rely on? Vs. 16

19. How is living in love and God living in us, one in the same? Vs. 16

20. In this world, who are we to be like? What is His chief attribute? Vs. 17

21. According to vs. 18, what are opposites?

22. What drives out fear? Vs. 18

23. What fears in your life do you need His perfect love to drive out?

24. Why do we love? Vs. 19

25. If you love God, what is out of character to do? Vs. 20

26. Simply put, if we love God, what must we do? Vs. 21

27. How has the Holy Spirit spoken to your life in this study?

CHAPTER 12
TELLING OTHERS THE GOOD NEWS

By now you are well aware of the word "Gospel." This word simply means "Good News." This news is nothing like you will hear on CNN or Fox. This is the only news which can liberate the human soul. To many the Gospel is not well received, but to others it's like a cup of cold water in a desert. It often depends on the spiritual readiness of the one hearing. When Christ called you, not only did you receive all these wonderful blessings, you also get to be a blessing to others. May His zeal for lost souls fill your heart and activate your life to service.

Read Luke 19:1-10

1. What kind of man was Zaccheus?

2. How did Jesus treat him?

3. How did Zaccheus respond?

4. According to vs. 10, why did Jesus come?

5. What image in your mind do you think of when you think of the word "lost?"

Read John 4:7-42

6. In your own words, describe how Jesus shared "Good news" with this woman. How did He break the ice? How did he treat her?

7. How did she respond?

8. What did Jesus say His food was?

9. What did He say about the harvest?

10. How did the city respond to the change in this woman?

Read Matthew 28:16-20

11. How much authority does Jesus have?

12. In vs. 19, what are we commanded to do?

13. What promise of Jesus helps to encourage us in this task? Vs. 20

Read Mark 16:15-18

14. What command is given here?

15. What promises are given to those who obey this command and believe?

Read Acts 1:8

16. When the Holy Spirit fills us with power, what is the purpose for this?

Read Philemon 1:6

17. By being active in sharing our faith, what blessing do we receive? *Read this in the NIV to understand the question.*

Read James 5:19-20

18. What happens when we help turn a sinner back from his ways?

Read II Corinthians 5:17-21

19. What happens to the one who is "in Christ?" Vs. 17

20. What ministry have we been given? Vs. 18

21. What does an Ambassador do? For example, how does the U.S. ambassador to India function? With what authority does he speak?

22. How does this relate to our ministry as Ambassadors?

23. What is our basic message? Vs. 20, 21

Read Colossians 4:2-6

24. In verses 3-4 what does the author (Paul) ask prayer for?

25. How are we to conduct ourselves in this world?

26. What should our speech be like?

27. What does it mean "To take advantage with every opportunity with outsiders?"

28. How can you effectively do this in your life?

God has called you to reach your "Circle of Influence"—list all your friends, neighbors, relatives, and co-workers who do not know Jesus.

How can you begin to influence their lives for Christ?

Keep this list in a place that will remind you to pray for them regularly.

CHAPTER 13
FRIENDSHIP WITH JESUS

Passion is a word with many different meanings. To one it may evoke a negative image and to another a picture of unending devotion. In our pursuit of God it is an entirely appropriate word. Without passion for God the believer never enters into the type of relationship God intends. A quick scan of scripture will reveal that every man or woman God used in a significant way had passion. In a few it was misguided, some had obvious flaws, but they always came back to passion for God. In this final lesson we will learn about being friends with God. Everything flows out of this relationship. After all, it is easier to live a godly life, evangelize, pray, and serve others when you are in love with the one you are serving.

Read Mark 12:28-31

1. This is known as the "Great Commandment." What is the essence of this command?

2. What must be first in our lives?

Read John 17:3

3. What is the essence of eternal life?

Note: The New Testament was originally written in the Greek language. In this language there were two words used for our English word, "know." They were "ginosko," and "oida." Ginosko describes an intimate knowledge, like a marriage relationship. Oida describes an intellectual knowledge, like reading a book. Oida reads the book, ginosko knows the Author. In John 17:3 and the next verse you will read that the word for know is ginosko.

Read Philippians 3:10

4. If you have a study Bible, try to find out when this book was written.

5. Was it near the beginning or end of Paul's life?

6. Since it was near the end, how significant is this prayer of Paul?

7. What two aspects of Christ's nature did Paul want to know?

8. Can you ever stop "knowing" Christ?

Read John 17:26

9. Read this verse carefully, and answer this question: To what degree can we love Jesus?

10. Make this verse a scripture you pray for yourself and other Christians on a regular basis.

Read Psalm 27

11. What seems to be the overall theme of this Psalm?

12. Look at verse 4, what one thing did David want more than anything?

13. Look at verse 8, when his heart encouraged him to seek the Lord, how did he respond?

14. How does this Psalm speak to you?

Read Psalm 42

15. In verse 1, how does his soul long for God?

16. In verse 2, what is the cry of his heart?

Read Psalm 63

17. What words are used in verse 1 to describe his hunger for God?

18. Have you ever been really thirsty for water? Can you imagine being this thirsty for God?

19. What is better than life? Vs. 3

20. How is his soul satisfied? Vs. 5

21. What did he often do on his bed? Vs. 6

22. If you could choose one word to describe this Psalm, what would it be?

Read Psalm 84

23. Write down as many blessings you can find for the man or woman who pursues God in this Psalm.

24. In verse 2, how did his soul react to the courts of the Lord?

25. Is it possible for both your heart and flesh to cry out for God?

26. In verse 5, what term is used to describe the life of the follower of God?

27. In verse 10, what was better to the author (Sons of Korah) of this Psalm than a thousand days anywhere else?

28. What would he have rather been, than to be wicked.

Read Psalm 101

This Psalm describes the home of the man or woman of God. It is a good reminder of how serious we must be in not allowing wickedness in our homes. But at the beginning you will find more of this passion for the Presence of God.

29. In verse 2, what question does David ask of the Lord?

30. How can this become, more and more the cry of your life?

31. With your friend or small group, (if you are going through this material with another Christian), determine when you will "meet with God."

REGISTER THIS BOOK

Get access to more study materials by visiting:

http://bit.ly/establishedinthegospel

ABOUT THE AUTHOR

Tom Elliott is a servant to the Body of Christ. He serves as Pastor of Life Church in Fort Collins, Colorado, is part of the leadership for Life for the Innocent (a ministry that rescues children from slavery in Asia), and oversees Life Leadership Academy, which trains pastors in Southeast Asia. Tom is committed to helping Christians make the focus of their walk with God the Person of Jesus (Hebrews 12:2) and is dedicated to helping them "overcome," rather than get by. He loves to help Christian leaders serve from a place of spiritual and emotional health and is committed to raising up as many leaders as possible, and empowering every person in the Church to disciple others. Tom has been married to Trenna since 1988, and they have three wonderful daughters (Elizabeth, Maria, and Rebekah).

OTHER BOOKS BY TOM ELLIOTT

http://jesusfocused.com/shop/

Grounded in the Word

Peace, success, relational skill, and eternal life are just some of the promises made to those who read and apply the teachings of the Bible. However, many misuse the Bible and treat it as a restaurant menu or a good luck charm. In order to experience the great promises made in the Bible it has to be properly navigated. That's the purpose of *Grounded in the Word*; to help you get the most out of this supernatural book. Did you know that the Bible is a gateway to experiencing God? The Bible is the only true "living document," because it's literature that gives life! God wants to reveal Himself to you and walk with you every day and the Bible is His gift to help you in this most noble quest.

Skillful Living
A 31-Day Devotional in Proverbs

Wisdom has been defined as "skillful living" and the Book Proverbs will help you live skillfully like few other works of literature. It contains 31 chapters and I have made it a practice to read the Book of Proverbs every year during one of the 31-day months. I invite you to do the same.

Many things have changed over the years and centuries, but human nature has never changed. The understanding of human nature is one of the most important lessons in life, and with this understanding will come great skill in living. Proverbs includes almost every person you will ever meet—both good and bad—and it addresses most of the choices we face in life.

This devotional is designed for you to read a chapter in Proverbs, write your personal thoughts and consider the brief commentary by the author. You may want to make notes of the different "types of people" you meet in this fascinating book. May God bless you, and make you Skillful at living!

Guided by the Holy Spirit

If you were determined to learn a new subject, would you want an average teacher or the best person in that field? If you were to set out on a hike through an unknown wilderness, would you want someone who had a little experience or the person who knew the land like his own house? The answers are obvious, right? What about this life, is it not filled with the constant need to learn and is it not a scary wilderness? You need a Teacher, and a Guide. If a person who really did know everything offered to be your Teacher and Guide in this life, would you take them up on the offer? The Holy Spirit is that Person.

The purpose of *Guided by the Holy Spirit* is to help you develop a deep friendship with the Holy Spirit. Friendships are deepened when we get to know the other person, share their interests, listen to them, and spend quality and quantity time together.

This book will help you learn how to accomplish all of these things effectively with the Holy Spirit. You are not alone, you have a friend and the Holy Spirit can be your best Friend.

OTHER BOOKS FROM
WALK WITH GOD PUBLISHING

Wake Up and Rest Series
By Thomas M. Mitchell

Wake Up and Rest—The Bride of Christ Sleeps at Her Own Peril... This book is a wakeup call to those who have made their personal commitment to their Lord and Savior Jesus Christ. They are the ones who hold the key to survival the world is looking for and they cannot fail to share it. But to do so they have to overcome their human side and allow their spirit to take charge and lead them through this "wilderness" we find ourselves in. And the key to that is to stop and take a long hard look at their relationship with the One to whom they're engaged to be married. Do we really know Him? What is He expecting of us? How can we find the answers? These questions and many more have to be answered if we're going to be able to step up and become all that He created us to be. *Wake Up and Rest* is a guidepost to a fruitful walk with our bridegroom as we prepare ourselves for our wedding day.

The Doorway to Rest—The Brides' Invitation... When we consider Solomon's Song—the love relationship he had with one of his wives—we can easily see the relationship between Christ and His bride portrayed. And that relationship has been portrayed in many ways. Think of the "sun's" relationship with the moon being like our relationship with the "Son." This book is a detailed, verse by verse study of the *Song of Solomon*, revealing the true view of bride of Christ through the eyes of the bridegroom and a life changing view of the bridegroom through the eyes of the bride.

The Pathway to Rest—The Brides' Purpose... Looking at the message of the *Song of Solomon* we were given a clear picture of not only who our bridegroom is, but equally important how He sees us and how we should see Him. His invitation opened the doorway to His Rest and now, as we walk out the days of our *ketubah*—our betrothal—we need to find out what that means and what it entails along the pathway to His Rest. For that we turn to the book of *Hebrews*, where we learn through each verse what sewing our wedding dress means and how important it is for us to be ready and watching for His soon return as we move up the path to spiritual maturity.

The Dangers to Rest—The Brides' Warning... We have been inundated with not the shout of triumph but the incessant worldly scream of pending disaster. The country's economics have been turned upside down and fear and panic have grabbed the headlines as the Middle East falls into chaos. The news is full of rampant pandemics, meteorological disasters, hopeless individuals committing tragic acts and families destroyed. And sadly, the majority of the bride of Christ is not prepared for His return. We have allowed the world and its supreme ruler to distract us from the path the lies in front of us. Now He has finally released me to write this verse-by-verse study out of the book of *Revelation* that He put on my heart 18 years ago concerning His letters that not only deal with why He is coming back but also what we, His bride, are supposed to be doing and not doing as we wait and watch.

The Battle for Rest—The Brides' Armor... Spiritual warfare is a war between the forces of God and the forces of rebellion led by Satan. And the bride is engaged in this spiritual war between light and darkness, good and evil, Heaven and Hell and Christ and

Satan. But sadly, many aren't even aware of the fact that they are in a spiritual battle every day of their life. As believing Christians we're in a grim conflict and not on a worldly cruise ship or a showboat; it's a battleship. It is a fight to the finish with no holds barred and we can't be neutral and we can't call a truce. And this war is a personal one; very personal. In this book we have taken a detailed verse-by-verse study of the part of the book of *Ephesians* that deals with the enemy, his strategies and his goals and most importantly the battle orders we have been given from our commander-in-chief to ensure victory over those personal strongholds the enemy has established in our lives.

The Way of Enoch Series
by Thomas M. Mitchell

In this series a door to a solid study of our foundation is opened by looking at our Walk With God in eight volumes. Each volume takes a look at a key fundamental part of our walk. They were written with the goal of challenging the bride of Christ to firm up her underpinning and step into the Spirit-filled, victorious and abundant life that Jesus has for her. And to accomplish that we need to draw near to Him through the leading of the Holy Spirit. Our Christian life should be spent with Jesus where He is now, in the Holiest Place. It's there that we will find His mercy and grace in the power of His blood. This series explores the foundation and sound scriptural doctrine that underlies God's plan for our lives. It is a journey beginning with learning who God really is and culminating with discovering how we are to walk out a loving and obedient relationship with our Creator.

Volume 1—*Your Life in Christ*
Volume 2—*The Spirit-Filled Christian*

Volume 3—*Foundations of Faith*
Volume 4—*The Word of God*
Volume 5—*Principles of Prayer*
Volume 6—*Authority of the Believer*
Volume 7—*Walk the Walk*
Volume 8—*The Obedient Lifestyle*

NOTES:

NOTES:

NOTES:

NOTES:

NOTES:

NOTES:

NOTES:

NOTES:

NOTES:

NOTES:

NOTES: